Choose Joy!

A journey through the book of Philippians
to discover the key to true joy

BY MARJIE SCHAEFER

www.FlourishThroughTheWord.com

© 2013 by Marjie Schaefer. All rights reserved. No part of this document may be reproduced or transmitted in any form by any means, electronic, mechanical, photocopying, recording, or otherwise, without prior written permission of Marjie Schaefer.

Dedication

I dedicate this Bible study on joy to my dear friend and mentor in the faith, Margaret Luke. Margaret has invested into me for over 25 years, sharing her wisdom and insight on prayer and God's Word. I have gleaned so much from watching her live for Jesus over the years, that I could fill a book! Her love for God and His Dear Son is consistently translated into her deep love for and ministry to His people, of which I am a grateful recipient. The most outstanding quality that has ministered to me over the years is Margaret's profound joy in Jesus. She has chosen the pathway of greatest fulfillment and joy by praising God every day, and this is evidenced in the overflow of her life. As Margaret says so often, "It's all about Him!"

I also dedicate this study on joy to my precious sister in Christ, Vickie Adair. Vickie has learned that praising God in a prison is the road to victory. She has come through a great trial in which she decided on the front end of that experience, that she would praise her Savior every day and for everything that touched her life. She knew that His Hand of love had allowed it, and by faith, she would choose joy. The fruit of her choice is evident to everyone who knows her. Vickie consistently radiates joy in Jesus, regardless of her circumstances. She is a trophy of His grace and her on-going witness for Christ blesses me every time I see her.

A Note from Marjie
BEFORE YOU BEGIN

Author William Barclay said, "It is only when truth is discovered that it is appropriated. When a man is simply told the truth, it remains external to him and he can quite easily forget it. When he is led to discover the truth himself, it becomes an integral part of him and he never forgets."

Truth applied transforms lives, and what we do everyday matters more than what we do once in a while. Through the study of *Choose Joy*, each person is given the opportunity to cultivate an appetite for more truth and more transformation. My prayer for each of you is that you will determine to daily 'mine the depths' of this study in order to tap into all of the treasures God has for you in His living and active Word.

Your personal time set aside each day to 'discover truth for yourself' will be the primary factor in how much you glean from the study of Paul's letter to the Philippians and his consistent message to 'choose joy'!

I also encourage you to daily set aside time to list out your specific reasons to rejoice. As you continually praise Him, you will discover more and more of an increase of God's Presence in your daily life because 'to praise God is to delight ourselves in Him.' (Psalm 37:4)

The study is designed to be done in a group setting where each person has done their individual homework, and then they come together to discuss their findings, to rejoice together, and to commit it all to prayer.

Praise Declarations
FROM SCRIPTURE

"I will bless the Lord at all times; His praise shall continually be in my mouth. My soul shall make its boast in the Lord; the humble shall hear of it and be glad. Oh magnify the Lord with me, and let us exalt His name together." Ps. 34:1-3

"I will sing to the Lord for He has triumphed gloriously! The Lord is my strength and my song, and He has become my salvation; He is my God and I will praise Him." Ex. 15: 1-2

"Let all those who seek You rejoice and be glad in You; let such as love Your salvation say continually: the Lord be magnified!" Ps. 40:16

"I will offer sacrifices of joy in His tabernacle, I will sing; yes, I will sing praises to the Lord!" Ps. 27:6

"Oh that men would praise the Lord for His goodness." Ps. 107:8

"The boundary lines have fallen for me in pleasant places." Ps. 16:6

"I will sing to the Lord for He has been good to me." Ps. 13:6

"Gracious is the Lord and righteous; yes, our God is merciful." Ps. 117:2

"Praise the Lord! Praise the Lord, O my soul! While I live will I praise the Lord. I will sing praises to my God while I have my being. Happy is he who has the God of Jacob for his help, whose hope is in the Lord his God." Ps. 146:1-5

"My lips shall utter praise, for You teach me Your statutes." Ps. 119: 171

"How great is Your goodness which You have laid up for those who fear You, which You have prepared for those who trust in You." Ps. 31:19

"For I proclaim the name of the Lord: Ascribe greatness to our God. He is the Rock; His work is perfect; for all His ways are justice. A God of truth and without injustice, righteous and upright is He." Deut. 32: 3-4

"Satisfy us in the morning with Your faithful love so that we may shout with joy and be glad all our days." Ps. 90: 14

"Let God arise and let His enemies be scattered; let those also who hate Him flee before Him. But let the righteous be glad; let them rejoice before God; yes, let them rejoice exceedingly. Sing to God, sing praises to His name." Ps. 68: 1, 3-4

"I will give You thanks in the great assembly; I will praise You among many people." Ps. 35:18

WHY WE NEED TO
Praise God More

Worshiping God is not just about singing praise songs in church once a week. Worship and praise is what we do in the car on the way to work, to school, or to the store. It's what we have in our heart when we're in the mall, the airport, or the doctor's office.

It's what we do when the kitchen sink stops up, the car has a flat tire, we become sick, or we've lost our keys for the millionth time. It's what we speak fervently when we are in the emergency room, at a loved one's burial, or in the middle of a storm. It's an on-going attitude of the heart. An attitude that doesn't change, no matter what else in your life does.

I'm not talking about some kind of positive thinking. This is not a plunge into denial.

I'm talking about looking at the reality of your life straight on and declaring an even greater reality straight over it.

Instead of letting yourself sink to the level of the problem, make yourself rise to the level of the solution.

One of the secrets of experiencing the power of praise is to make a decision that you will worship God no matter what your circumstances are. When you get to the place where praise comes automatically, no matter what is going on, you will come to know God more intimately. And when you do, you won't be able to stop yourself from praising Him.

When we make our first reaction to what happens in our lives a reaffirming praise to God for who He is, we invite His presence to inhabit the situation and His power to come and change things. This is the hidden power of praising God.

God wants you to exalt Him and not your problems. The more you praise Him, the more you are centered on Him and the more you will be relieved of the burden of those problems. This doesn't mean you are pretending they do not exist. It means you are saying, "Although I have these problems, I know that You Lord, are greater than they are. You created me. You are my heavenly Father. You are a good God. In You is everything I need for my life, and I choose to exalt You above all."

When you become convinced of the power of praise in every situation, and understand all that is accomplished when you are a true worshiper of God, your life will be changed forever.

~ Stormie Omartian from the book,
<u>The Prayer that Changes Everything</u> p. 16-17

Choose Joy!
WEEK 1

"Fill thou my life, O Lord my God
In every heart with praise,
That my whole being may proclaim
Thy being and Thy ways."

~Horatio Bonar

Joy in Living

WEEK 1: Day 1

 Review notes from the teaching session.
Read the entire chapter: Philippians 1:1-30.

1. What new thing did you learn about or what impacted you regarding:

    The book of Philippians and its background?

    Paul?

    Praising God?

    Prayer for others?

    Be ready to share any of these insights with your group.

2. Read verses 7-11.

    According to this passage, how did Paul feel about the Philippian believers?

    What kind of practical application can we draw from Paul's life and example of how he related to others?

    Briefly scan the entire letter of Philippians and write down the names of the people who Paul mentions, (you should have seven.) What do you learn about Paul and people?

What is the Holy Spirit saying to you through this passage regarding your relationships in the body of Christ?

3. Read verses 9-11 in two or three translations if you can.

    The Message Bible is provided for you here:
    "So this is my prayer: that your love will flourish and that you will not only love much but well. Learn to love appropriately. You need to use your head and test your feelings so that your love is sincere and intelligent, not sentimental gush. Live a lover's life, circumspect and exemplary, a life Jesus will be proud of: bountiful in fruits from the soul, making Jesus Christ attractive to all, getting everyone involved in the glory and praise of God."

    Read and study the Greek words and definitions:

    Pray: *__proseuchomai__*- Strong's #4336 –a progressive word that starts with a noun which is a prayer to God, expands to a verb describing a request or entreaty. Jesus said in Matthew 6:6: "<u>When</u> you <u>pray</u>…"

    Love: *__agape__*- Strong's #26 –Christianity gave new meaning to this word; an undefeatable benevolence; good will that always seeks the highest good of the other no matter what he/she does; self-giving love that gives freely without asking for anything in return; it is not based on the worth of the object.

    Abounding: *__perisseuo__* –Strong's #4052 –To super abound; have excess; greatly surpass.

    Sincere: Pure: *__eilikrines__* –Strong's #1506 –Literally 'tested by sunlight' –exposure of any flaws; free from falsehood; pure; without hidden motives.

    Righteousness: *__dikaiosune__* –Strong's #1343 –Just; the quality of being right; conformity to the will of God in all respects; both judicial and gracious.

    Praise: *__epainos__* –Strong's #1868 –Commendation and approval.

DO: Personalize this prayer using the Greek definitions and different translations to expand and expound on Paul's prayer for the Philippians. Space has been provided for you here:

⚷ Your challenge is to use this prayer throughout the remainder of this study as you intercede for others.

⚷ Be prepared to share your prayer with your group and to pray it with your group for one another.

> "Living agape is a daily commitment
> of the will to vacate the premises
> of the heart with its own preferential
> affections, and to make its chambers a
> fleshly canteen for the liquid love of God."
> ~ Beth Moore, *Believing God Day by Day*

Christ is Preached

WEEK 1: Day 2

 **Read:** Philippians 1:12-18

1. How did God use Paul's imprisonment to further the Gospel? Be specific.

2. What has happened in the course of *your* life that God has used for the furtherance of the Gospel? Give a specific example/story from your life.

3. In verse 13, Paul proclaims that his "chains are in Christ." What do you think this means in light of the context and remembering the story of Acts 16?

4. What specific examples do we have today of fellow believers whose "chains are in Christ?"

5. Paul told of others, in verse 16, who were preaching Christ from **selfish ambition**: Being concerned with your own welfare; an ambitious, self-willed person seeking opportunities for promotion; a partisan spirit; one who would use any method to win favor or followers.

In Philippians 2:3, Paul exhorts, "Let nothing be done through <u>selfish</u> <u>ambition</u> or conceit, but in lowliness of mind let each esteem others better than himself."

Based on the specific information given in verses 16-18, what was the <u>result</u> of those who preached out of selfish ambition?

What conclusion can you draw from this?

How did Paul <u>choose</u> to respond to the "ambitious" people?

How can you personally apply Paul's response and conclusions to your current circumstance, whatever they may be?

Personal 🗝

Has the Holy Spirit "pricked" you in any way in this lesson regarding selfish ambition? Take some time to converse with God about this.

To live is Christ!

WEEK 1: Day 3

Read: Philippians 1:19-26

1. What two things did Paul state (v. 19) would help with his deliverance?

2. What three things did Paul earnestly hope for according to verse 20?

3. Describe how Paul felt about living and dying based on his recorded thoughts in vs. 21-24.

4. What were some of the "pros" (versus "cons") of staying alive?

5. What are some practical applications you can glean from Paul (vs. 21-24) in regards to how we are to live and how we are to think? (Give verse) EXAMPLE: Do not fear death because being in heaven with Jesus will be amazing! (v. 21)

6. What things can you summarize from these verses (19-26) that you can pray for yourself and for others?

7. Take some time to go back over your personalized prayer written from Day 1 and pray this for anyone the Lord has put on your heart.

Striving for Christ

WEEK 1: Day 4

 Read: Philippians 1:27-30

"Let your conduct be worthy of the Gospel…" (NKJV)

"Meanwhile, live in such a way that you are a credit to the message of Christ." (The Message)

1. What does this command mean for you in your day to day living? Use other Scriptures to support your answer, and give specific examples.

2. Paul continues in verse 27, that he wants to hear of their affairs, standing fast in one spirit, with one mind striving together…

   Compare this Scripture with Ephesians 4:1-6 and Jude 3. Explain what these commands mean for you and for all of us as part of the Body of Christ. Be very practical with your answer.

Look up Philippians11:28 in two or three translations if possible. I have provided the verse for you in The Philips Translation:

"The fact that they are your enemies is plain proof that they are lost to God, while the fact that you have such men as enemies is plain proof that you yourselves are being saved by God."

4. Compare this with Romans 8:37; Psalms 25:2; II Corinthians 2:14. From this brief study, summarize the message Paul is giving to the Philippians in your own words.

5. What are the two things granted to believers in v. 29? How does Paul handle his "conflict" based on what you see in your study of chapter one? What is a dominant theme of Paul's life? Use the passage in Acts 17:2-3 and the Greek word for suffer to help you answer this.

Suffer: *pascho* –Strong's #3958 – "To experience ill-treatment, roughness, violence, or outrage; to endure suffering and to undergo evils from without. It appears 42 times and is mostly used to refer to Christ's sufferings for us. "

Take My Life

*Take my life and let it be
Consecrated, Lord, to Thee.*

*Take my moments and my days;
Let them flow in ceaseless praise.*

*Take my hands, and let them move
At the impulse of Thy love.*

*Take my feet and let them be
Swift and "beautiful" for Thee.*

*Take my voice, and let me sing
Always, only, for my King.*

*Take my lips, and let them be
Filled with messages from Thee.*

Rejoice Journal

"Rejoice in the Lord always. Again I will say, Rejoice!"
PHILIPPIANS 4:4

- Record things, people, events that you are rejoicing over.

- Record Scriptures that proclaim the power of rejoicing from your study.

Choose Joy!
WEEK 2

"Rightly understood, every truth in God's Word leads us to Jesus."
~Charles Spurgeon

Unity Through Humility

WEEK 2: Day 1

Read: Philippians 2:1-4

1. The apostle Paul was deeply committed to spiritual unity. He told the Philippians that they would fulfill his joy if they would be "like-minded", of "one accord," and "of one mind." This is consistent with the prayer of Jesus and the experience of the early church, and the teachings of the apostles.

    Using the Greek definitions below and the other Scripture references, provide a working definition of unity, in your own words, that reflects Paul's message of unity to the Philippian Christians in verses 1-4.

    Consolation/Comfort –*paraklesis* –Strong's #3874 –a calling, alongside, to help, to comfort, to give consolation or encouragement. The paraklete is a strengthening presence –one who holds up those needing help.

    Fellowship –*koinonia* –Strong's #2842 –Sharing unity, close association, partnership –unity brought about by the Holy Spirit where individuals share common bonds of fellowship in the Christian community. *Koinonia* is the "glue" that holds believers to Jesus and to each other.

    John 17:20-23

    Acts 2:42-47

    Ephesians 4:3-6

    I Peter 3:8

2. How does unity in the church impact the spread of the Gospel?

3. "If you've gotten anything at all out of following Christ, if his love has made any difference in your life, if being in a community of the Spirit means anything to you, if you have a heart, if you care -then do me a favor: Agree with each other, love each other, be deep-spirited friends. Don't push your way to the front; don't sweet-talk your way to the top. Put yourself aside, and help others get ahead. Don't be obsessed with getting your own advantage. Forget yourselves long enough to lend a helping hand." (MSG) Philippians 2:1-4

   Using the two Greek definitions below and looking up the related Scriptures, tell what it <u>means</u> and what it <u>looks</u> like to live out verses 3-4 of this Scriptural command.

   Selfish ambition –*eritheia* –Strong's #2052 –A person concerned only with his own welfare, a person susceptible to being bribed, an ambitious, self-willed person seeking opportunities for promotion.

   Humility –*taprinophrosume* –Strong's #5012 –Modesty, lowliness, humble-mindedness, and a humble attitude of unselfish concern for the welfare of others. Total absence of arrogance, conceit and haughtiness.

   Galatians 5:26

   Romans 12:10

   Acts 20:19

   I Corinthians 13:5

   Romans 15:1-2

4. Can you share a personal testimony of how you have been blessed by or ministered to by someone's unselfish care of you and your interests?

5. Is there a practical or tangible way you can 'look out for the interests' of another this week? Who is on your heart? Is there someone the Lord keeps bringing to mind? Share with someone in your group this week what the Lord prompted you to do.

6. Go back to week 1, chapter one and the prayer you wrote out from verses 9-11. Pray and intercede for others using that prayer this week.

Joy in the Humbled & Exalted Christ

WEEK 2: Day 2

Read: Philippians 2:5-11

Read this passage over several times and in several translations if possible. Keep in mind as you study this passage (Historically described as the most sublime passage of the whole New Testament) that Paul's reason for writing was _unity_.

1. Read verse 5. Look up related verses and write down the principle you glean from each verse:

    Matthew 11:29

    I Corinthians 11:1

    I Peter 2:21

    John 5:30

    John 5:44

    Summarize what you have briefly investigated and state what it means to have the mind of Christ –or to let this mind be in you. How do you get it? How do you maintain it?

2. Read verse 6. When Paul refers to the 'form of God,' the word 'form' comes from the Greek word **morphe**. It is used only three times in the New Testament –twice being in this section. Look up Hebrews 1:3 and II Corinthians 4:4, Hebrews 4:15 and I John 2:2

What do you learn from these verses and how does it apply or relate to verse 6?

What do you think is the key idea of verse 6?

Why is it important to understand this as a Christian?

How does this relate to humility?

3. Read verse 7. Jesus gave up the right to Himself (Romans 15:3.) Look up these Scriptures and summarize them.

    I Corinthians 6:19-20:

    John 1:14

    John 5:30

    John 4:34

    Galatians 1:10

If Jesus did not come to do His own will, and gave up rights to Himself, how does this relate practically to us?

What would it mean for you to 'make yourself of no reputation?'

How can you tell if you have a servant attitude?

4. What do we learn about Jesus from these verses?

John 5:19

Mark 1:35

Luke 5:16

Luke 6:12

Matthew 8:20

Joy in the Humbled & Exalted Christ

WEEK 2: Day 3

 Reread: Philippians 2:5-11

1. Read verse 8. Paul wants to convey to his readers the words 'in appearance,' refers to the fact that Jesus had a certain presence. He could be seen and recognized by anybody –it did not take a spiritual person to see or hear Him.

   John referred to this too: "That which was from the beginning, which we have heard, which we have seen with our eyes, which we have looked at and our hands have touched –this we proclaim concerning the Word (Jesus) of Life." (I John 1:1)

   Read the following verses and list the facts or characteristics you see about Jesus.

   Hebrews 2:10

   Hebrews 4:15

   Hebrews 5:7-8

   Luke 22:41-44

   In Philippians 2:8, what two actions did Jesus deliberately take?

If Jesus was perfect, why do you think He humbled Himself?

Record what you learn from James 4:6 and 10 and I Peter 5:5-6. Do you naturally humble yourself and submit the process?

To what degree are you prepared to be obedient?

2. Read verse 9. Christ being exalted to the highest position, an elevation above all others, is a direct result of His humbling Himself and His obedience of death of the cross. In the Kingdom of God, the way up is down. Promotion is from the Lord.

These verses describe the exaltation of Christ. List out some facts that you learn from these passages (bullet points):

    Hebrews 2:9

    Acts 2:32-36

    Ephesians 1:20-23

What exactly is the 'name which is above every name?'

3. Read verses 10-11. There is power in the name of Jesus and every knee <u>will</u> bow in submission to Him.

   See John 12:12-13. **Name** –*onoma* –Strong's #3686 –Name or term by which a person or thing is called. In Hebrew and Greek times, a name also implied authority or rank, character, reputation and representation.

   Cross reference Isaiah 45: 23 to see Paul's bold declaration. (Write out)

   Read Acts 4:12 and John 13:13 and list what is stated here in these verses.

   From your own knowledge of the Scriptures, list as many names for Christ that you are aware of. Many are found in the Gospel of John (The Way, The Truth, The Life.) Write them here and please try to list the references with them.

4. Go back and review the two day's study of this passage, keeping in mind that Paul's purpose in writing was unity in the Body of Christ. What do you see as the over-arching emphasis or application for all of us as members of the Body of Christ?

Meekness and majesty, manhood and deity,
In perfect harmony, the Man who is God:
Lord of eternity dwells in humanity,
Kneels in humility and washes our feet.
Father's pure radiance, perfect in innocence,
Yet learns obedience to death on a cross
Suffering to give us life,
Conquering through sacrifice,
And as they crucify, prays, "Father, forgive."
Wisdom unsearchable, God the invisible,
Love indestructible in frailty appears.
Lord of infinity, stooping so tenderly,
Lifts our humanity to the heights of His throne.
what a mystery, meekness and majesty:
Bow down and worship, for this is your God,
This is your God!

~Graham Kendrick

Joy in Being a Light
WEEK 2: Day 4

 Read: Philippians 2:12-18

1. Read and record your insights from the following verses and Greek definitions:

    John 6:27, 29

    Luke 19:9

    I John 4:18

    Hebrews 13:20-21

    I Thessalonians 2:13

    Philippians 1:5-6

Obey –*hupakouo* –Strong's #5219 –To hear as a subordinate; listen attentively, obey as a subject; answer and respond, submit without reservation –hearing –responding and obeying

Salvation –*soteria*- Strong's 4991 –Deliverance, preservation, soundness, prosperity, happiness, rescue, well-being. Salvation is a present possessive and future realization.

Works –**effectively**-*energeo* –Strong's 1754 –Active operation or working of power and its effectual results.

What does it mean to 'work out your own salvation?' based upon your study?

How do we do this? Is it up to us?

Is this a 'works' righteousness? Why or why not?

How do we participate in the process? (Be practical)

Is Paul contradicting himself by telling us to work out our own salvation and then saying it is God who works in us?

2. Verse 14 is a powerful verse! Look up some related Scriptures on what we do with our mouths and write out a principle you glean for each:

   Luke 6:45

   Proverbs 18:21

   I Peter 3:8-10

   Proverbs 15:4

   Proverbs 21:23

   How are we to 'do everything' without complaining? What is the key to living out this verse and obeying it consistently? Read John 5:19 for some insight.

   Do you think this is part of 'working out' our salvation?

3. Jump ahead to Philippians 4:8 and read this verse. This is Paul telling us specifically what we are to think about. Compare Philippians 4:8 to Luke 6:45.

   What is the abundance of the heart?

   How can we regulate our hearts and our mouths?

   How does Philippians 4:13 help us to understand and practice this command?

   "I have strength for all things in Christ Who empowers me [I am ready for anything and equal to anything through Him Who infuses inner strength into me; I am self-sufficient in Christ's sufficiency]." Philippians 4:13 Amplified

   Paul tells us that if we do all things without complaining, we will become:

   _____, _____, children of _____,

   without_____,

   shining as _____.

"Complaining is praising the enemy"

"The longer I live, the more I realize the impact of attitude on life. Attitude, to me, is more important than facts. It is more important than the past, than education, than money, than circumstances, than failures, than successes, than what other people think or say or do. It is more important that appearance, giftedness or skill. It will make or break a company...a school...a home. The remarkable thing is we have a choice every day regarding the attitude we will embrace for that day. We cannot change our past... we cannot change the fact that people will act in a certain way. We cannot change the inevitable. The only thing we can do is plan on the one thing we have, and that is our attitude...
I am convinced that life is 10% what happens to me and 90% how react to it."

–Charles Swindoll

4. What action does Paul tell us to take in verse 16? How do we do that and what does it mean?

   Word –*logos* –Strong's #3056 –a transmission of thought, communication, a word of explanation, an utterance, divine revelation, divine promise, divine doctrine.

   Jesus is the living *Logos* –
   "In the beginning was the Word..." John 1:1

   The Bible is the written *Logos* – "The Word of God is living and powerful..." Hebrews 4:12

   The Holy Spirit utters the spoken *Logos* – "These things we also speak, not in words which man's wisdom teaches but which the

Holy Spirit teaches, comparing spiritual things with spiritual."
I Corinthians 2:13

Personal 🗝

What place does the 'word of life' have in your life?

"The Bible is the only book in the world that when you read it, the Author shows up!"

What do you see of Paul's attitude in verses 16-18?

Review and pray the intercessory prayer from chapter one.

Joy in Christian Fellowship
WEEK 2: Day 5

 Read: Philippians 2:19-30

1. Read this passage where Paul shares about Timothy and Epaphroditus. Timothy often functioned as Paul's personal envoy, "For this reason I have sent Timothy to you, who is my beloved and faithful son in the Lord, who will remind you of my ways in Christ, as I teach everywhere in every church." I Corinthians 4:17. List the qualities Paul writes about each one in the chart below:

Paul	Timothy

What do you learn from this simple investigative study that you can apply to the relationships in your life?

Who is the "Paul" in your life? Who is speaking into your life?

Who is your "Timothy"? Is there someone you are mentoring or investing in?

Have you ever prayed for God to send you His choice of Christian friends?

Is your character proven by those who know you, work with you, minister with you?

How does one get "proven character?

Integrity
is what you are when
no one's looking!

Rejoice Journal

"Rejoice in the Lord always. Again I will say, Rejoice!"

PHILIPPIANS 4:4

- Record things, people, events that you are rejoicing over.

- Record Scriptures that proclaim the power of rejoicing from your study.

Choose Joy!
WEEK 3

"All the words of men and angels could not fully set forth the greatness of the grace of our Redeemer. Trust Him! Make a running leap into His arms. Venture on Him, venture wholly; let no other trust intrude."

~Charles Spurgeon

Joy in Giving All for Christ
WEEK 3: Day 1

Read: Philippians 3:1-11

Paul is beginning to 'wrap up' his letter here using the word 'finally' in verse 1. 'Finally,' or as the message Bible says, "And that's about it friends." Paul tells us that the duty of all Christians is that they be joyful. The Greek meaning for rejoice is to be cheerful, calmly happy, glad.

"A long-faced Christian is the worst advertisement against Christianity." –Dr. Henrietta Mears

1. How can a Christian be joyful in a world full of sorrows according to verse 1? (See also I Thessalonians 5:16)

    Why do you think Paul would say writing these things over and over was a safeguard?

    Philippians 4:13 in the Amplified Version states:

    "I am ready for anything and equal to anything through Him Who infuses inner strength into me; I am self-sufficient in Christ's sufficiency."

    How does this verse help you to understand and apply the command to be joyful?

    How are you putting this into practice?

What have you learned about rejoicing in the Lord at this point in your journey through Philippians?

In verses 2 and 3, Paul warns the believers against Judaizers, or legalists, who insisted on and taught that strict observance of the law was necessary for salvation. The Legalists taught that circumcision was paramount, and this teaching continually came against the gospel of free grace. The reality Paul was expressing here is that a physical ritual without righteousness of heart is nothing more than mutilation of the flesh.

2. Paul emphasized that worship for the Christians (those who had their hearts circumcised) is in the Spirit, rejoicing only in the finished work of Christ on the cross, and not a work of the flesh. Look up the related Scriptures and list principles of true worship in the Spirit, without dependence on anything else:

   Galatians 6:15

   2 Corinthians 5:17

   Colossians 1:15

   Colossians 3:16

   John 4:23-24

   Summarize what you glean from these verses and Paul's message.

Look up these Scriptures and list three characteristics of worshipping God in the Spirit:

Ephesians 5:18-19

I Corinthians 14:15

I Corinthians 14:1-2

What have you learned about true Christian worship from the Scriptures that maybe you had not seen before?

3. In verses 4-5, Paul gives somewhat of a resume along with his personal testimony of how he now sees his life's accomplishments because of Christ. What did Paul specifically say about how he felt/thoughts about his former gains in verses 7 and 8?

Personal 🗝

If you were to list out your "Christian resume," what would you write down that you have done for God?

Looking at your list, honestly and prayerfully ask the Lord to search your heart to see if you put 'confidence in' (v. 4) anything other than Christ, His Word, and His Spirit at work in you, no matter how noble. (This is meant to be a cleansing time, not a condemnation of anything.)

What, if anything, can you 'throw away' for the sake of knowing Christ in a deeper way? Would you be willing to give up aspects of your life with its comforts, for the sake of experiencing deeper communion with Christ? (Like sleep for instance?) What would that look like for you?

Joy in the Possession of the Priceless Privilege

WEEK 3: Day 2

Read: Philippians 3:8-12

When Paul encountered the Lord on the road to Damascus, his entire life –internally and externally –was dramatically transformed (Read Acts 9:1-30 for the story.) As we saw last time, he discovered in Christ a store of spiritual wealth that made him count all he had built his life on before as "rubbish" (Philippians 3:8).

1. Read verses 8-12 and note especially verse 8 in the Amplified version:

    "Yes, furthermore, I count everything as loss compared to the possession of the priceless privilege (the overwhelming preciousness, the surpassing worth, and supreme advantage) of knowing Christ Jesus my Lord and of progressively becoming more deeply and intimately acquainted with Him [of perceiving and recognizing and understanding Him more fully and clearly]. For His sake I have lost everything and consider it all to be mere rubbish (refuse, dregs), in order that I may win (gain) Christ (the Anointed One)."

    List out from these verses some of the ambitions or desires of Paul's heart. List the verses next to it. The first one is done for you.

    > v.8 –Paul wanted to gain Christ
    >
    > v.9 –
    >
    > v.9 –

v.10 –

v.10 –

v.10 –

v.10 –

v.11 –

v.12 –

2. Paul knew that the only thing that ultimately counted in life was knowing the Lord and being obedient to His will.

   Read Paul's stated life purpose in the Amplified Bible:

   Verse 10: "For my determined purpose is that I may know Him [that I may progressively become more deeply and intimately acquainted with Him, perceiving and recognizing and understanding the wonders of His Person more strongly and more clearly], and that I may in that same way come to know the power outflowing from His resurrection [which it exerts over believers], and that I may so share His sufferings as to be continually transformed [in spirit into His likeness even] to His death…"

   This is where you will end your study today. Your challenge is to do several things with this verse:

   Type or write this verse out (Amplified version please) on a 3x5 card and place it in your Bible, at your kitchen sink, in your car, or on your bathroom mirror –somewhere prominent where you will see it often during the day.

   Make this your prayer, several times throughout the rest of the week, several times a day.

Personal 🗝

Prayerfully ask yourself, 'Can I agree with Paul that this is my life purpose too? What am I doing to 'progressively become more deeply and intimately acquainted with Him?"

Have you come to a place in your Christian pilgrimage where you have a 'life purpose' determined by God, and you can articulate this purpose with a Scripture? If so, use this space to write it out.

Joy in Pressing Forward

WEEK 3: Day 3

Read: Philippians 3:13-16

1. Read verse 13. Name the two specific and deliberate things Paul does in this verse:

   _____

   _____

   How do Paul's attitude and actions square with what Jesus said in Luke 9:62?

   What do you think of Paul, church-planter, missionary, New Testament author, claiming that he had not "apprehended" all the things God had for Him to do yet?

   What was Paul looking at, according to verse 14?

   In light of verse 14, and the surrounding context, and Hebrews 3:1, what do you think is the upward call of God?

How have you responded to that call in your life?

What are some ways that the Holy Spirit is prompting you to press on and reach forward towards the goals God has for you?

What will you do about obeying these promptings?

Is there a close friend or family member who can hold you accountable? Remember: "If you aim at nothing, you will hit nothing."

2. Read verse 15 along with I Corinthians 2:6-16. List out several points from the Corinthian epistle of how God "reveals" His mind and wisdom to us:

3. Read verse 16 and compare it with Romans 12:16 and Romans 15:5-6.

   What is the benefit of being like-minded with other believers?

   What are some ways that you could grow in this area?

   Formulate your findings into a prayer based on these three Scripture references.

Joy in Our Blessed Hope
WEEK 3: Day 4

 Read: Philippians 3:17-21

Earlier we learned about the Judaizers who were maligning the gospel of grace with their demand for strict keeping of the law. In addition, other carnal believers were infiltrating the Philippian church by promoting a perversion of Christian liberty and using it as a license to sin. Here Paul had some practical advice for his fellow brothers and sisters: Imitate me!
(Additional references: I Corinthians 4:16 and 11:1)

1. In verse 17, Paul lists three aspects of combating sinfulness; what are they?

    1.

    2.

    3.

2. In verse 18, what does Paul call these 'lawless' ones and how is he feeling about them?

    Questions for personal reflection and application:

    Can others imitate your life and devotional "patterns" because you are imitating Christ? How so? What about your life in Jesus? Could you pass it on to others?

Do you have any current enemies that are also "enemies of the cross of Christ"? If so, what has been your response?

3. In verse 19, list the four things these enemies of the cross live for:

   1.

   2.

   3.

   4.

   What is the antidote (given in verse 20) to the self-centered, fleshly lifestyle?

   How are we to wait for Jesus?

How does a life that imitates Christ reflect our gratitude to Him?

Describe the 'Extreme Home Makeover' that will occur for us when Jesus comes (v.21)!

Rejoice Journal

"Rejoice in the Lord always. Again I will say, Rejoice!"

PHILIPPIANS 4:4

🗝 Record things, people, events that you are rejoicing over.

🗝 Record Scriptures that proclaim the power of rejoicing from your study.

Choose Joy!
WEEK 4

"He asks nothing of us,
but that we ask
everything of Him."
~Charles Spurgeon

Ultimate Joy In Christ Our Strength

WEEK 4: Day 1

Read: Philippians 4:1-5

The blessed hope of Christ's return and our eternal life with Him, casts its gracious influence and JOY over all of life. Paul prays that believers will have joy at all times and not be worried by cares. The way to be anxious about nothing is to be prayerful about everything –with thanksgiving! We are encouraged to put our prayers into God's hands and go off and leave them there. Do not worry about them. Give them completely as the farmer gives the wheat to the soil after the soil has been properly plowed. If we do this, then the peace of God will stand guard over our hearts and minds.

1. In verse 1, Paul begins with the word 'therefore.' Why is it there for? Review the previous verses in chapter 3 and describe the context and the reason why Paul gives this exhortation. Turn back to Philippians 1:2 and see Paul's same command to _____ _____. What does it mean to stand fast in the Lord?

In verses 2-3, Paul specifically calls out two women who are at odds with each other (how embarrassing!) They caused dissension in the church. Paul was determined to have them unified, and he called on the whole church to get involved! Disruptions in the unity of the church are a very serious matter because they disrupt the flow of the Gospel. Paul was passionate about unity in God's House and among God's people.

What do you learn about Euodia and Syntyche in this brief report?

Read Paul's teaching on unity in Ephesians 4:1-6. List out the characteristics of unity from this passage.

2. Contextually, two dynamics that feed unity in the Body of Christ are consistent rejoicing and *gentleness*, according to verses 4-5.

In verse 4, is Paul presenting rejoicing as an option for believers?

Why are we to rejoice always? Use Romans 12:12 as a help to answering this question and also, your entire journey through Philippians so far (remembering our blessed hope in chapter 3).

How does this verse and Philippians 2:14 relate to each other?

3. Paul also wrote another letter and issued a similar command. Read I Thessalonians 5:16-19. List out the commands given by Paul:

   1.

   2.

   3.

   4.

   What does Paul say we can know with certainty in verse 18?

4. We are commanded in I Thessalonians 5:19 not to quench the Spirit. How does this command of what we are *not to do*, connect to the previous three commands of *what we are to do*?

Have you ever sensed that the Holy Spirit was quenched in your life? Describe what that was like.

How do we quench the Holy Spirit? (See Ephesians 4:29-31 for the answer.) List some of the ways.

5. Paul is very specific about our rejoicing. What/who are we to rejoice in?

How is this different from rejoicing in circumstances?

How can a Christian rejoice, even in the midst of extremely difficult or even tragic circumstances? To help you answer, use the following Scriptures:

Philippians 4:12

Habakkuk 3:17-18

2 Corinthians 6:4-10

What do you call worship/rejoicing when you don't feel like it?

6. Look up these verses on what the Bible has to say about praise:

    Deuteronomy 10:21

    Psalm 22:3

    Isaiah 64:5

    Does this motivate you to praise Him?

    List out some great and awesome things your eyes have seen the Lord do in your own life.

    Share some specific ways He has 'met you' in your rejoicing.

7. Read Psalm 34. List out several words or expressions used to describe praise.

List out the benefits you see in this Psalm as a result of praising and crying out to God.

Did the Lord show you anything new from this Psalm?

8. In Phil.4:5, Paul says we are to be known for our _____. Why do you think Paul says this should characterize our lives as believers?

Joy in Praying

WEEK 4: Day 2

Read: Philippians 4:6

"Do you know, believers, what great things are to be had for the asking? Have you ever thought about it? Does it not motivate you to pray fervently? All of heaven lies within the grasp of the asking individual. All the promises of God are rich and inexhaustible, and their fulfillment is to be had by prayer. Jesus said, "All things are delivered unto me of my Father" (Matthew 11:27), and Paul said, "All things are yours…and ye are Christ's" (I Corinthians 3:21, 23). Who would not pray when all things are handed over to us like this? Promises that were first made to specific individuals are also made to us if we know how to plead them in prayer. For example, only Jacob was present at Peniel, yet Hosea used the word *us* in referring to the experience: "There he spoke with us" (Hosea 12:4). Israel went through the Red Sea ages ago, yet the word *we* is used in the sixty-sixth Psalm: "There did we rejoice in him" (v. 6).

When Paul wanted to give us a great promise for times of need, he used these words: "for he hath said, I will never leave thee, nor forsake thee" (Hebrews 13:5). Where did Paul get that verse? It was the assurance that the Lord gave to Joshua: "I will not fail thee, nor forsake thee" (Joshua 1:5). You may think, "Surely the promise was for Joshua only. "No, it is for us. "No prophecy of the Scripture is of any private interpretation" (II Peter 1:20). All Scripture is ours. God is waiting to be gracious and load us with His benefits. If we ask, God will give us much more than we ask. Prayer is the great door of spiritual blessing, and if we close it, we shut out His favor."

~Charles Spurgeon, <u>Praying Successfully</u>

1. We arrive at the well-known, oft-quoted verse 6 of Philippians 4. Paul issues the command to "Be anxious for nothing." The way is also given to off-set worry: Pray! Pray about everything. Everything can be affected by prayer.

   Read this verse in several translations.

   What are the three actions we are to take in verse 6:

   A.

   B.

   C.

   A. The first action is to be anxious for nothing. Look up the following verses that issue a similar command along with the Greek words and definitions. Summarize each verse and what you have learned about not worrying:

   Psalm 55:22

   Matthew 6:25-36

   1 Peter 5:7

Sustain: Hebrew –*chul* –Strong's #3557 –To maintain, nourish, provide food, bear, hold up, protect, support, defend, to supply the means necessary for living.

Worry: *merimnao* –Strong's #3309 –To divide into parts, a distraction, a preoccupation with things causing anxiety, stress, and pressure.

Care: *merimna* –Strong's #3308 –To be anxious beforehand about daily life.

B. The second directive in verse 6 is to pray –ask of God. Look up other verses that the Bible provides in regards to praying and asking. Write out a principle you learn from each verse.

    Matthew 7:7-11

    Psalm 50:15

    James 4:2-3

    James 4:8

    Ephesians 3:20

    John 16:24

    John 15:7

C. The third active aspect of verse 6 is to ask with thanksgiving. This is stated in two different ways in the following Scriptures:

    I Thessalonians 5:17-18

    Colossians 3:15

Look up these verses and summarize the conclusions you make between asking God and spontaneously thanking Him.

2. In verse 7, an automatic "fruit" or result of obeying verse 6 in sequence is the peace of God, guarding our hearts. The Greek word for 'guard' is a military term that pictures a sentry standing guard as protection against the enemy.

Re-visit Colossians 3:15. What are we to do in this verse?

Look up I Peter 1:5 and discover another aspect of being 'guarded' or kept –what keeps you?

What did Jesus leave us with in John 14:27?

Why did Jesus come according to Luke 1:79?

Peace in the Greek denotes a state of rest, quietness, calmness, absence of strife, tranquility and includes harmonious relationships. So we are commanded to "let the peace of Christ rule in our hearts," and Isaiah 26:3 gives us a very practical way to do that: _____.

3. This brings us to verse 8, which re-emphasizes the principle of Isaiah 26:3. We are told what we should think about because right living begins with right thinking.

   List out each of the eight "whatever things" we are to deliberately think on, and give a definition of each and how you are to 'work this out' in your own life.

   1.

   2.

   3.

   4.

   5.

   6.

   7.

   8.

   How do you practically meditate on these things?

Paul tells us four ways that he taught the Philippians:

1.

2.

3.

4.

How is it that he made these four things separate and distinct? How is it possible to hear but not receive?

What is the promised outcome of the Philippian believers "doing" what Paul taught them?

Why do you think Paul stressed the peace of God so much in this section?

Practical Application 🗝

Try this tangible exercise:

*Get a few pieces of blank paper.

*On each piece, write down anything you may be anxious about or anything that may be robbing you of your peace.

*Prayerfully go through each piece of paper and each item, giving it to the Lord and leaving it with Him.

*After you do this, rip up each piece of paper and throw them away!

WEEK 4: Day 3

Read: Philippians 4:10-12

1. In verse 10, what is Paul rejoicing about? (Use Philippians 2:25 and 4:14-16)

   What do you learn about the Philippian Christians from these verses?

2. Verses 11-12 are the very familiar and 'famous' quotes on contentment. Answer the following questions:

   Where was Paul as he wrote the words "I have learned in whatever state I am to be content?"

   How do you think, based on your personal study of Philippians, that you learn contentment in prison? (To answer, review Philippians 2:14; 3:1; 4:4)

   What additional principles do you learn from Paul's advice to Timothy in I Timothy 6:6-8?

When you read a verse like Hebrews 13:5, how do you reconcile that with new things you may be asking God to do or bring into your life? (Review John 15:7-8). Be sure and discuss this in your groups.

In 2 Corinthians 9:8, Paul is speaking a word of testimony out of his own life. How does the "abundance" he speaks of in this verse, align with the testimony he gives in Philippians 4:12 regarding hunger and need?

3. From the whole of Scripture, it is obvious that Paul had seasons of abundance and seasons of extreme material/physical need, yet he learned contentment in each season. As each season providentially arrived in his life, he derived as much good as he possibly could from the lessons God brought His way.

Have you had seasons of need in your own walk with the Lord? How has the Lord provided for you in those seasons and what were some personal lessons you gleaned from those times?

4. How about seasons of abundance in your life? What have you learned from those times?

5. How are we to view each season? (Use Philippians 4:11 to help you answer)

Joy in Dependence

WEEK 4: Day 4

Read: Philippians 4:13-20

The context of these remaining verses in Philippians 4 is dealing with Paul's need as he is in prison for serving the Lord. Earlier he gave testimony to how he had learned to be content in any and every situation –in plenty or in need. His joy remained firmly fixed <u>in the Lord</u> and not his circumstances.

Verse 13 is a powerful and pivotal verse in this passage. The emphasis is not on Paul's <u>achievements</u> but on his <u>willingness to depend</u> on the power of Jesus to sustain him in confinement or freedom, in abundance or scarcity. This is called relying on the grace of God.

"I have strength for all things in Christ who empowers me. I am ready for anything and equal to anything through Him who infuses inner strength into me; I am self-sufficient in Christ's sufficiency." Amplified

"Whatever I have, wherever I am, I can make it through anything in the One who makes me who I am". The Message Bible.

Paul obviously understood grace. Grace teaches us that God is inclined to help us in our weakness and in our failure. God sees our inability as reality, and He is not mad at our vulnerabilities. Grace is knowing God is for us.

"Our weakness makes room for God's power." ~Jim Cymbala

"Grace that leads to true life transformation is one of unmerited favor –the understanding that <u>God is truly for us</u> and that He will provide what we cannot provide for ourselves (Phil. 4:13). Grace means we receive the gifts we need for growth to occur. We don't 'willpower' our way there." ~Dr. Henry Cloud

"Every <u>limitation</u> we have can be seen as an <u>invitation</u> from God to do for us what we cannot do for ourselves." ~ Stephen Arterburn

Grace is God's gift to you. He offers new life based on nothing you have to offer. There is not a way to earn His affections or care for you. He sees your sin, does not excuse it, but loves you anyway. He delights in you and befriends you. He is compassionate and has the capacity to be intimately involved in your life.

1. What has historically been your understanding of grace?

2. Look up Hebrews 4:16 and compare the context and substance of this verse with Philippians 4:13. What two things are we to receive based on your study of Hebrews 4:16.

3. What does John 15:5 teach us about grace and dependence? How does this verse resonate with Philippians 4:13?

4. The balance of this passage deals with Paul's need and the Philippians' generosity and care of him. Read verses 14-19 and list out all the facts you glean from this section (in bullet points) regarding the Philippians' generosity.

Verse 17 states that Paul sought the fruit that abounds to their account. What does he mean by that? Look up Titus 3:14 and share your insights from this verse and how it relates to Paul's statement.

For some final principles on handling abundance and giving to others, look up the following Scripture and state what you learn from each one:

I Timothy 6:17

Jeremiah 9:23-24

Ecclesiastes 5:18-19

John 10:10

5. Relate all of these to the glorious promise of Philippians 4:19.

6. Paul ends his letter to the Philippians the same way he started it. How?

7. After your in-depth, verse-by-verse study of this delightful book, why do you think Paul ends with grace? Why is this important?

Amazing grace, how sweet the sound,

That saved a wretch like me.

I once was lost, but now am found,

Was blind, but now I see!

~John Newton

Rejoice Journal

"Rejoice in the Lord always. Again I will say, Rejoice!"

PHILIPPIANS 4:4

🔑 Today, re-visit your previous 4 weeks of study and rejoicing. What has been your big 'take-away' from your journey through Philippians?

🔑 How was your life changed?

Now that you've finished.....

I hope that you enjoyed your study of God's Word through <u>Choose Joy</u>. I am always amazed at the new things I learn from verses I've read my entire life. That's what makes God's Word so fresh and relevant. He even tells us in the Bible that every verse of Scripture is profitable (see 2Timothy 3:16). So if you did even a portion of this study, your time in the Word was profitable.

I encourage you to stay connected to this study by continuing to record in the 'rejoice journal' as part of your daily routine. Go back and re-visit the highlights from this study or the things that meant the most to you. God has revealed Himself to you in a deeper way through your incremental and inductive study of this entire book. When He gives you a word of instruction, He also gives you the power to accomplish it. You can step out in bold faith and *'choose joy'* each day, knowing that God backs up every word He utters.

You never lose by being in God's Word! Here's a verse that proves it: "God rewrote the text of my life when I opened the book of my heart to His eyes." (Psalm 18:24 MSG)

To God be all the glory!
– Marjie

About the Author

Marjie Schaefer was born in Georgia, raised in Texas and has spent the past 3 decades in Washington state. She and her husband, Steve, have been married for over 25 years and have 4 children: daughter Hayley, and sons Jordan, Matthew and Luke. Marjie has had the privilege of being a stay-at-home mom for the past 23 years and considers this a great blessing.

Marjie describes herself as an everyday girl who loves Jesus and daily pursues a life with Him at the center of her activities and purposes. She started leading and teaching Bible studies while a student at Washington State University, and has continued to open her home and her life to anyone who wants more of the Word and more of Jesus. Her greatest passion is bringing the Word of God to life through practical application and visual tools. Women look forward to her personal touches while attending her studies, and they usually go home with laminated verses and other tangible reminders of God's love for them.

Marjie started spending deliberate and daily time in the Word of God while she was a young girl at the encouragement of her godly mother. This has given her a foundation that has stood the test of time. She began writing her own Bible studies at the request of some friends who desired to study the Word during the summer months. *Grace Encounters*, a Bible study that chronicles the interactions of Jesus with five different women, is available at Amazon.com.

If you want to stay current with Marjie and the Bible-teaching ministry she is a part of, Flourish Through the Word Ministries, go to her website at www.marjieschaefer.com or find Flourish Through the Word on Facebook. You can also follow Marjie on Twitter @followmarjie.

Bibliography

Unless otherwise noted, Scripture quotations are taken from the Holy Bible, New King James Version, Spirit-Filled Life Bible, Copyright 2002, by Thomas Nelson Publishing, Nashville, TN.

Scripture quotations designated Message are taken from The Message Bible by Eugene Peterson. Copyright 1993, NavPress Publishing Group.

Scripture quotations designated Amplified are taken from The Amplified Bible, Copyright 1987, by Zondervan Corporation.

Scripture quotations designated Phillips Translation are from The New Testament in Modern English by J. B. Phillips, Copyright 1958, Macmillan Publishing.

Other resources used for research, information, context and background:

The Bare Bones Bible Handbook, by Jim George, Copyright 2006, Published by Harvest House Publishing.

Handbook to the Bible, Eerdman's, Copyright 1973, Lion Publishing.

What The Bible Is All About Bible Handbook, Dr. Henrietta Mears, Copyright 1953, Regal Publishing.

Imitating Christ, R.T. Kendall, Copyright 2007, Charisma Publishing.

Just Say Thanks! R. T. Kendall, Copyright 2005, Charisma House.

The Prayer That Changes Everything, Stormie Omartian, Copyright 2004, Harvest House Publishers.

A Distant Presence: the story behind Paul's letter to the Philippians, Tim Woodroof, Copyright 2001, NavPress.

Praying Successfully, Charles Spurgeon, Copyright 1997, Whitaker House Publishing.

Lose It For Life, Stephen Arterburn, Linda Mintle, Copyright 2004, Integrity Publishers.

www.ingramcontent.com/pod-product-compliance
Lightning Source LLC
Chambersburg PA
CBHW070549300426
44113CB00011B/1838